MINTY

• A Story of Young Harriet Tubman •

by ALAN SCHROEDER   pictures by JERRY PINKNEY

PUFFIN BOOKS

For my parents, Walt and Hilda Schroeder, with love —A.S.

In memory of my mother, Williemae,
and Charles L. Blockson,
friend and preserver of history —J.P.

PUFFIN BOOKS
Published by the Penguin Group
Penguin Putnam Books for Young Readers, 345 Hudson Street, New York, New York 10014, U.S.A.
Penguin Books Ltd, 27 Wrights Lane, London W8 5TZ, England
Penguin Books Australia Ltd, Ringwood, Victoria, Australia
Penguin Books Canada Ltd, 10 Alcorn Avenue, Toronto, Ontario, Canada M4V 3B2
Penguin Books (N.Z.) Ltd, 182-190 Wairau Road, Auckland 10, New Zealand

Penguin Books Ltd, Registered Offices: Harmondsworth, Middlesex, England

First published in the United States of America by Dial Books for Young Readers,
a member of Penguin Putnam Inc., 1996
Published by Puffin Books, a division of Penguin Putnam Books for Young Readers, 2000

1 3 5 7 9 10 8 6 4 2

THE LIBRARY OF CONGRESS HAS CATALOGED THE DIAL EDITION AS FOLLOWS:
Schroeder, Alan.
Minty: a story of young Harriet Tubman / by Alan Schroeder
pictures by Jerry Pinkney.—1st ed.
p. cm.
Summary / Young Harriet Tubman, whose childhood name was Minty,
dreams of escaping slavery on the Brodas plantation in the late 1820s.
ISBN 0-8037-1888-8 (trade)—ISBN 0-8037-1889-6 (lib. bdg.)
1. Tubman, Harriet, 1820(?)–1913—Childhood and youth—Juvenile literature.
2. Slaves—United States—Biography—Juvenile literature. 3. Afro-Americans—Biography—Juvenile literature.
4. Underground railroad—Juvenile literature. 5. Antislavery movements—United States—Juvenile literature.
[1. Tubman, Harriet, 1820?–1913. 2. Slaves. 3. Afro-Americans—Biography. 4. Underground railroad.]
I. Pinkney, Jerry, ill. II. Title.
E444.T82S37 1996
305.567'092—dc20 [B] 95-23499 CIP AC

Puffin Books ISBN 0-14-056196-X

Printed in the United States of America

The full-color artwork was prepared with pencil, colored pencils, and watercolor.

While *Minty* is a fictional account of Harriet Tubman's childhood, and some scenes have been invented for narrative purposes, the basic facts are true. Harriet Tubman—whose "cradle" name was Araminta (hence the nickname, Minty)—was indeed a slave on the Brodas plantation on Maryland's Eastern Shore in the 1820's. She was known as a "difficult" slave, and was often punished for it. As in this story, Minty was sent to work in the fields after proving herself too clumsy and not docile enough to be a house slave. Further, she was assigned, on one occasion, to tend to muskrat traps; it's easy to imagine that it was in her nature to free a captured animal, just as she would one day help to free hundreds of slaves. —A.S.

The challenge that *Minty* initially posed for me came from not having a clear picture of Harriet Tubman's early childhood. However, I was able to imagine the spirited eight-year-old Minty, using Alan Schroeder's strong text and Harriet Tubman's biography, *The Moses of Her People,* as springboards. The National Park Service was also helpful—I had just finished an assignment for them for the Booker T. Washington National Monument in Virginia—as was the Banneker-Douglass Museum in Maryland, where extensive research uncovered the style of plantations around Maryland during Minty's childhood and authentic details regarding backgrounds, dress, food, and living conditions of the enslaved as well as the slave owners. My interest was to give some sense of Minty's noble spirit and open a window to understanding the day-to-day, sunup to sundown life of the slave, by individualizing the hardships in overwhelming circumstances.

In 1978 I was privileged to create the first Harriet Tubman commemorative stamp for the U.S. Postal Service. This book, then, brings me full circle with Harriet's life and courage. —J.P.

"Minty! I know you hear me. Get in here, gal!"

Crouching in front of the big barn door, Minty listened. Mrs. Brodas sounded angrier than usual.

"Get in here, I said! Don't make me come and get you!"

Minty giggled, and then stuck out her tongue just as far as it could go. I'll come when I'm good and ready, she thought. But she didn't dare say it, not out loud. That would mean a whipping for sure.

Pushing back the barn door, Minty crept inside. The barn was her favorite hiding place.

The dray horses watched, restless, as Minty thrust her arms into a large pile of fresh hay. She dug deep down, all the way to the bottom, and pulled out her rag doll. Esther Lavinia Louise was a sorry sight, with one foot missing and a pair of cracked buttons for eyes. But Minty loved her just the same.

"Now listen," she said. Then, in a low voice, Minty started to tell an old Bible story, the way her mother had told it to her.

"And then the shepherd boy—David—he picked up this tiny little rock, took aim, and sent it flyin'. Hit the ol' master smack in the head. Killed him, right there in front of everyone. Then they had a big ol' party afterward, and David got to move into this big house with a long table, and he was never hungry or nothin' again."

When the story was finished, Minty hid Esther back at the bottom of the haystack. It was getting dark, and she had to light the fire, trim the wicks, and set the table up at the big house.

That evening at supper, Mrs. Brodas was still angry. "Why didn't you come earlier when I called? I had a mess of peas that needed shelling."

Minty looked down at her feet. "I didn't hear any call."

"Don't lie to me, girl, 'less you want a whippin'. Next time, you better jump to when I call." Mrs. Brodas shook out her cloth napkin. "I'm hungry. Serve the potatoes."

As Minty reached for the bowl, she accidentally knocked over a pitcher of cider. Mrs. Brodas jumped to her feet. "Now look what you've done!" Angrily, she turned to her husband. "Do you see, Edward? It's spite, pure and simple! Well, I won't stand for it. I don't want her in the house anymore. From now on, she's a field slave. That'll fix her." Then, crossing the room, Mrs. Brodas opened one of the high cupboards and took something out.

Minty's eyes widened. It was her rag doll, Esther.

"You didn't think I knew, did you?" said Mrs. Brodas. "Here," she told her husband, "take this and throw it in the fire."

"No, Missus!" Minty screamed. She lunged forward, but Mrs. Brodas was faster. With a flick of her wrist, she hurled the doll into the open fireplace. Minty kicked and screamed, but Mrs. Brodas held her back until the doll was nothing but a pile of white ashes.

"That'll learn you," she said. "Now get out of here. And don't forget—you're a field slave now."

Minty ran out, choking back her tears.

Later that night, while her brothers and sisters slept, Minty told her mother and father what had happened. "Well," said Old Ben, "at least they're keepin' you on. What if they'd sold you South? I've seen 'em do it for less than spillin' a pitcher o' cider."

Old Rit put aside her sewing. "Come here, girl," she said. "There's somethin' I got to say t' you." Minty laid her head down on Old Rit's lap. It was soft and warm, and she liked feeling her mother's hand as it ran gently across her forehead. "Listen to me, Minty. Now that you're in the fields, you gotta do a good job, 'cause there ain't no other place for them to send you but downriver—and you don't want that. Once they sell you South, you'll never come back."

"I'm gonna run away," Minty mumbled. "I am."

Old Rit shook her head. "Oh, no you're not. That's what you always say, and it ain't never gonna happen. You know what my daddy done tol' me? 'If your head is in the lion's mouth, it's best to pat him a little.' Your head's in his mouth, Minty, but you sure ain't doin' any pattin'. You're just fixin' to get your head bit off." Old Rit bent down to whisper. "Pat the lion, Minty. It ain't gonna kill you."

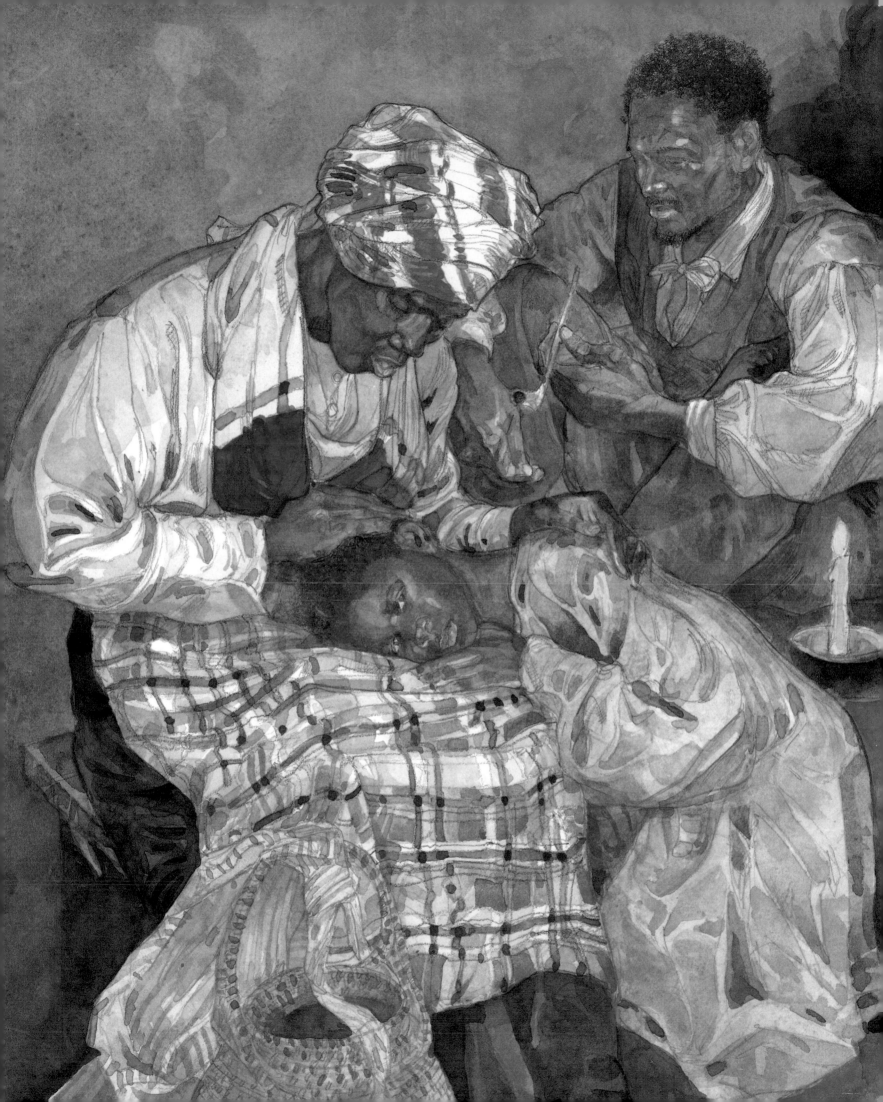

The next morning at dawn, Minty was sent to work in the fields. For the next few months, her job was to plant wheat and rye, and tend to the young corn. It was hard and heavy work, but Minty liked being outside. The breeze felt good on her forehead, and sometimes, when no one was looking, she'd push her toes deep down into the dirt and pretend she was a sunflower, rising up, up, up, all the way up till she could see clear across the Chesapeake Bay, till she could touch the clear, blue sky.

Then July came, and with it the heat and the mosquitoes. Some days Minty could hardly see what she was doing, she had so much sweat dripping down into her eyes.

"You oughtta wear a bandanna," said the woman next to her. "Say, you're a little 'un. How old are you, anyway?"

"I'm eight," said Minty.

The woman smiled, holding out her hand. "My name's Amanda."

"My name's Minty."

"That's a pretty name," Amanda said. "Real pretty."

"Be quiet," said the overseer, knocking the butt of his whip against his glossy, black boot.

Amanda lowered her voice to a whisper. "Tell your mama to make you a bandanna, or, girl, you gonna fry your brains out."

Whenever she was working in the fields, Minty kept looking for a way to escape. The dirt road behind the barn led to the Choptank River, but Minty had no idea where the river went. And what if there were snakes in the water? Minty was scared of snakes.

"I know what you're thinkin'," Amanda whispered. "I can see it in your eyes. You're fixin' to run away, but they'll catch you—and when they do…" She pointed to a deep scar on her forehead. "Believe me, honey, I've tried it and it ain't worth it. Uh-uh."

Later that day, the overseer, Sanders, rode up on his horse and pointed at Minty. "You," he said, "come with me."

Running behind, Minty followed him down the trail to the Big Buckwater River. There, next to the bank, she saw a thick rope stretched across the surface of the water. "Get in," Sanders ordered.

"But I can't swim," Minty said. "And, mist'r, it's cold."

"Don't sass me, girl. I said get in there! And take hold of that rope." He watched as Minty waded into the water. "You see those traps, the steel ones? Those are muskrat traps. Mr. Brodas wants you to check every one, and if there's a muskrat caught, you stuff 'im in here." The overseer thrust a heavy sack at Minty, then spat into the water. "Don't you get any ideas now," he warned. "Remember—I got eyes in the back of my head." Then, spurring his horse, Sanders galloped off.

Slowly Minty started downstream, holding tight to the rope.

The first two traps were empty, but inside the third, a fat, glossy muskrat was struggling to get free. Squatting down, Minty pulled apart the steel jaws of the trap. She glanced back to make sure Sanders was out of sight. Then, happily, she let the muskrat go, releasing it downstream. It swam away vigorously, propelling itself through the water with its long, flat tail. Minty's eyes were wide with excitement. "Go!" she cried, splashing at the water. "Go, swim away!"

She hurried to the next trap and did the same thing, releasing a second muskrat into the cold, muddy river. She was prying open a third trap when she heard a soft noise behind her. Sanders was sitting on his horse, not ten feet away.

For a long moment, he and Minty stared at each other. Then, suddenly, Minty dropped the trap and started to run. Sanders caught up with her at once. Jumping down, he bound her wrists together with a short piece of twine.

"That was a stupid thing to do," he said. "You'll be sorry, gal."

He took her back to the big house, where Mrs. Brodas was on the porch cracking walnuts. She listened to what Sanders had to say. Minty never got a chance to speak for herself.

"Whip her," Mrs. Brodas ordered. "Whip her good. And if it happens one more time, you tell my husband, hear? We'll sell her South. They'll know what to do with her in Georgia."

The overseer tied Minty to the fence. Then, roughly, he ripped open the back of her shirt. Old Rit was watching from a distance. As soon as she saw Sanders raise the whip, she dropped to the ground, her hands over her ears. "Oh, Lord, let it be quick," she moaned. "Let it be quick! Please, dear God, let it be over!"

Later, by candlelight, Old Rit did what she could to help Minty get through the night. "Now, this'll hurt some," she said, smearing green salve on Minty's back. "Oh, baby, don't cry. Don't do it. Here, bite down on this—it'll help." She forced a hickory stick between Minty's teeth. "I told you not t' aggravate 'em. I *told* you. Why didn't you listen, Minty? Don't you got any sense?"

It was several days before Minty could walk again. Then early one morning, she was sent back to the fields, where the rye and wheat stood tall. But Amanda was no longer there. Minty learned she'd been "sold South."

"And you're next," Sanders told her. "I got my eye on you."

That evening, Minty told her father that she was going to run away. "I mean it this time," she said.

"Oh, I believe you. Only problem is, you don't know where you're runnin' to." Old Ben rose from his chair. "Come outside, Minty. There's somethin' I want to show you." Silently they walked toward the barn. Old Ben lit his pipe, then pointed up at the sky. "Do you see that star?" he asked. "The bright one? That's the North Star, Minty. And do you see all those stars next to it?" With his finger, he traced the outline of the Big Dipper. "That's the Drinking Gourd," he said. "Now, you listen to me. If you're gonna run, first of all you make sure it's night—the darker the better. And before you do anythin' else, you look up and find the North Star. It'll be the only marker you'll have, so don't lose it." Old Ben reached for Minty's hand. "You follow that star," he said, "and it'll take you north, all the way to Philadelphia."

Minty looked up at the dome of the sky. To her, all the tiny stars looked alike. "Show me again," she said.

Old Ben pulled her close and, with the stem of his pipe, began painting a picture of freedom in the clear night sky.

The next morning, Old Ben told Rit that every Sunday he was going to take Minty into the woods. "If she's planning to run away, there's some things she oughtta know first." Rit didn't like the idea one bit—she was scared—but Old Ben told her to stay out of it. "I know what I'm doin'," he said.

One of the first things he taught Minty was how to read a tree. "If you're ever lost," he said, "and you don't know which way is north, just look at the moss growing on a tree. It always grows on the north side. Can you remember that?"

Minty nodded. Then she stretched out her fingers to touch the yellow-green moss. It felt fuzzy and a little brittle. She scraped some off the bark.

"Don't eat it," Ben warned. "It'll make you sick as a dog."

That summer, deep in the forest, Minty learned how to catch and skin a squirrel. She learned to do birdcalls, and before long, she could run barefoot through the woods without making a sound. She learned how to catch fish with nothing more than a piece of string and a bent nail. And in the still, muddy waters of the creek, Old Ben taught her how to swim.

"That's right," he said. "Keep your head down. Don't move your arms so much. You're doin' fine."

The only thing Minty couldn't learn was how to start a fire. Old Ben watched as she struck at the flint, trying to get a spark. "Just keep at it," he told her. "You'll get the hang of it."

On the last day of summer, Old Ben and Minty took a tin bucket into the forest and filled it to the top with blackberries. Then they climbed a hill overlooking the river and watched the sunset. By the time they got back to the cabin, it was already dark.

Old Rit put her hand into the bucket and laughed. "I know just what to do with these," she said, pouring the plump berries into a big wooden bowl. "Minty, you go up to the big house and ask Missus for some sugar and two cups of flour. Tell her I want to make a pie, if she'll let me. Go on now—and you hurry back."

Her bare legs shivering, Minty started up the dirt path. The night air was cool; autumn was coming on.

She had nearly reached the big house when she saw a buckskin mare tied to an oak tree out front. Minty figured it belonged to a guest, someone visiting the Brodases. The horse stood very still, watching her with uneasy eyes. Minty was about to turn away when a thought suddenly occurred to her. Reaching up, she placed her hand on the saddle. It was still warm—and not too high….

This is it, she said to herself. This is my chance to run away! Remembering what Old Ben had told her, she looked up at the sky. There it was, the North Star, shining bright.

By now, Minty's heart was beating rapidly. She wanted to run back to tell Old Ben and Old Rit good-bye, but she knew there was no time. It was now or never.

Holding her breath, Minty reached for the rope. She tried to untie the knot, but her hands were shaking badly. The horse let out a nervous whinny.

"Ssh," Minty whispered. "Don't be afraid." But it was her own fear that was growing. Then, just as the knot started to come undone, the door of the big house opened. Minty heard her master's voice.

"Come outside, Nathaniel. We'll have a smoke."

At that moment, Minty lost her courage. She couldn't do it. Not now. Not tonight. With tears in her eyes, she ran back down the hill to the cabin.

At the door, Old Rit caught her by the shoulder. "Where's the flour? What did Missus say?"

But Minty pulled away and wouldn't answer.

"Leave her be," said Ben. "Just leave her be, Rit. I'll fetch the flour."

That night, after everyone else was asleep, Minty sat next to the fire, thinking. Why, why hadn't she jumped on the buckskin? She could be long gone by now, halfway to Philadelphia. She might never get the chance again.

Minty began to cry. She cried for a long time, until the fire had nearly burnt itself out. It was getting cold in the cabin, and to keep warm, she buried her toes in the ashes at the edge of the pit. Up at the big house, a dog started to bark. Old Rit stirred in her sleep. Minty sniffled, then she wiped her nose with the back of her hand.

But someday...someday she would run away. She would jump on the buckskin's back and ride, ride, ride, the north wind whipping through her hair, and nothing would stop her. Nothing.

Minty could feel her eyes beginning to close. Then, little by little, she fell asleep. Curled up between her brothers and sisters, she dreamed of sunflowers and stars, and the call of the whippoorwill, and a road through the forest that one day, when she had the courage, would carry her to freedom....

Author's Note

It took many years, but Minty's dream came true. In 1844, when she was about twenty-four, she married a free black man named John Tubman. Five years later, in 1849, Harriet Tubman made a daring and successful escape from the Brodas plantation in Maryland.

"There was one of two things I had a *right* to," she said, "liberty or death; if I could not have one, I would have the other; for no man should take me alive; I should fight for my liberty as long as my strength lasted. . . ."

Traveling by night, Harriet Tubman made her way to Philadelphia, where she found a job in the kitchen of a hotel. But more than anything, she wanted to free others, just as she had freed herself. In 1850 she made the first of a series of perilous journeys back to the Eastern Shore of Maryland. There, at great personal risk, she helped hundreds of slaves (including members of her own family) escape north. Along the way, wherever possible, these fugitives were hidden in "safe" houses or barns owned by abolitionists, people who were opposed to slavery. This route of escape, which Harriet came to know well, was called the Underground Railroad. It was not underground, nor were there any trains or tracks, but the Railroad carried former slaves north to such cities as Philadelphia and New York, and from there across the border to Canada.

"I never ran my train off the track," Harriet said proudly, "and I never lost a passenger." For her daring and tireless work as a conductor on the Underground Railroad, Tubman is remembered as one of the bravest and most admired women in American history.

They called her "Minty."

When she grew up, she became Harriet Tubman, the courageous and heroic woman who helped hundreds of slaves escape to freedom through the Underground Railroad. But she was just a little girl for a while—and this is her story. Minty, short for Araminta, was a feisty and headstrong young slave, whose rebellious spirit often got her into trouble. She told stories to her doll, released animals from traps, and, above all, dreamed of running away. And when her father began to teach her the skills necessary for escape, she listened carefully, and learned. . . .

♦"Rich with melodrama, suspense, pathos, and, of course, a powerful vision of freedom. This exquisitely crafted book resonates well beyond its few pages."
—*Kirkus Reviews,* pointer review

WINNER OF THE CORETTA SCOTT KING AWARD
AN ALA NOTABLE BOOK

A PUFFIN BOOK
Ages 5–9
U.S.A. $6.99
CAN. $9.99

ISBN 0-14-056196-X

90000>

9 780140 561968

EAN

VISIT US AT www.penguinputnam.com/yreaders